SIMPLY**SCIENCE**

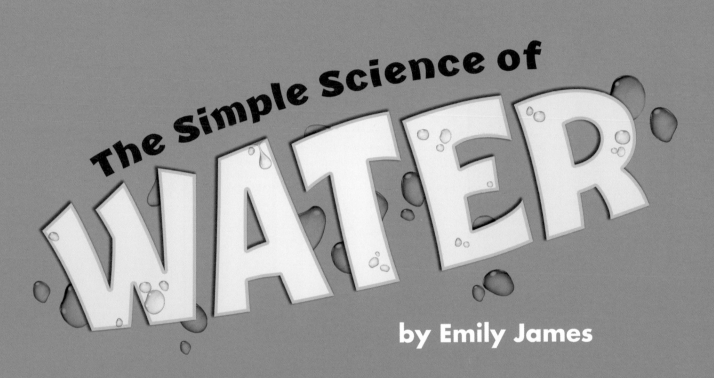

The Simple Science of

WATER

by Emily James

CAPSTONE PRESS
a capstone imprint

A+ Books are published by Capstone Press,
1710 Roe Crest Drive, North Mankato, Minnesota 56003
www.mycapstone.com

Library of Congress Cataloging-in-Publication Data
Cataloging-in-publication information is on file with the Library of Congress.

ISBN 978-1-5157-7080-0 (library binding)
ISBN 978-1-5157-7087-9 (paperback)
ISBN 978-1-5157-7094-7 (eBook PDF)

Editorial Credits
Jaclyn Jaycox, editor; Jenny Bergstrom, designer; Jo Miller, media researcher; Tori Abraham, production specialist

Photo Credits
Dreamstime: Woraphon Banchobdi, 4–5; Shutterstock: Adam Gryko, 13, all_about_people, 23 (inset), Brocreative, 27 (inset), Chris Byrne, 10, Foodpictures, 29 (inset), greenland, 26–27, Guniva, 20, Liam Huber, 12, Mclek, 16–17, Merkushev Vasiliy, 6–7, Monkey Business Images, 18–19, MrPhotoMania, 22–23, Mysikrysa, 21, PHOTOCREO Michal Bednarek, 8–9, robert_s, back cover, Sashkin, 14–15, Serg64, cover, Triff, 28–29, Trong Nguyen, 11, VAKSMAN VOLODYMYR, 19 (inset), Victoria Mende, 24–25

Design Elements
Shutterstock: 31moonlight31, Sermsak Winikun, StudioSmart

Note to Parents, Teachers, and Librarians

This Simply Science book uses full color photographs and a nonfiction format to introduce the concept of water. *The Simple Science of Water* is designed to be read aloud to a pre-reader or to be read independently by an early reader. Photographs help listeners and early readers understand the text and concepts discussed. The book encourages further learning by including the following sections: Table of Contents, Glossary, Read More, Internet Sites, Critical Thinking Questions, and Index. Early readers may need assistance using these features.

Printed in the United States of America.
010374F17

Table of
CONTENTS

**Where Do Raindrops
Come From?** 4

The Water Cycle 6

What Is Water Made Of? 14

Where Is Water Found? 16

What Is Water Used For? 18

Drinking Water 22

Sharing Water 26

Change It Up! 28

Glossary 30

Read More 31

Internet Sites 31

**Critical Thinking
Questions** 32

Index 32

Where Do Raindrops Come From?

Drip, drop. Drip, drop. Raindrops are falling! Where do they come from?

These raindrops have floated in a cloud.
They have traveled underground. They have
flowed down a stream. These raindrops have
been all around the world!

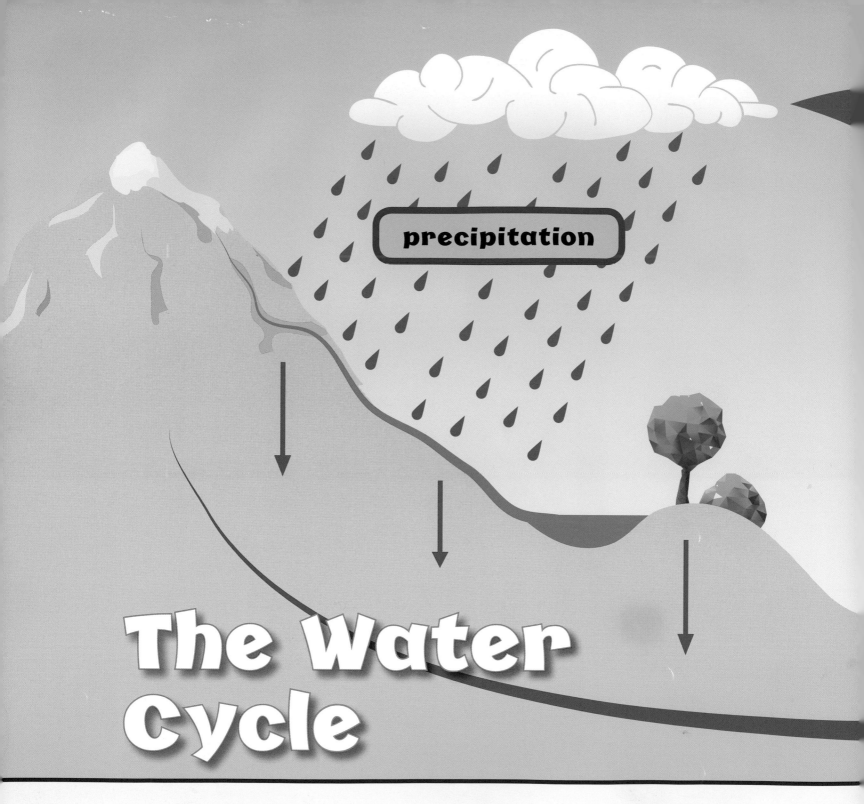

precipitation

The Water Cycle

Raindrops are made of water that
has been used over and over again.
They are part of Earth's water cycle.

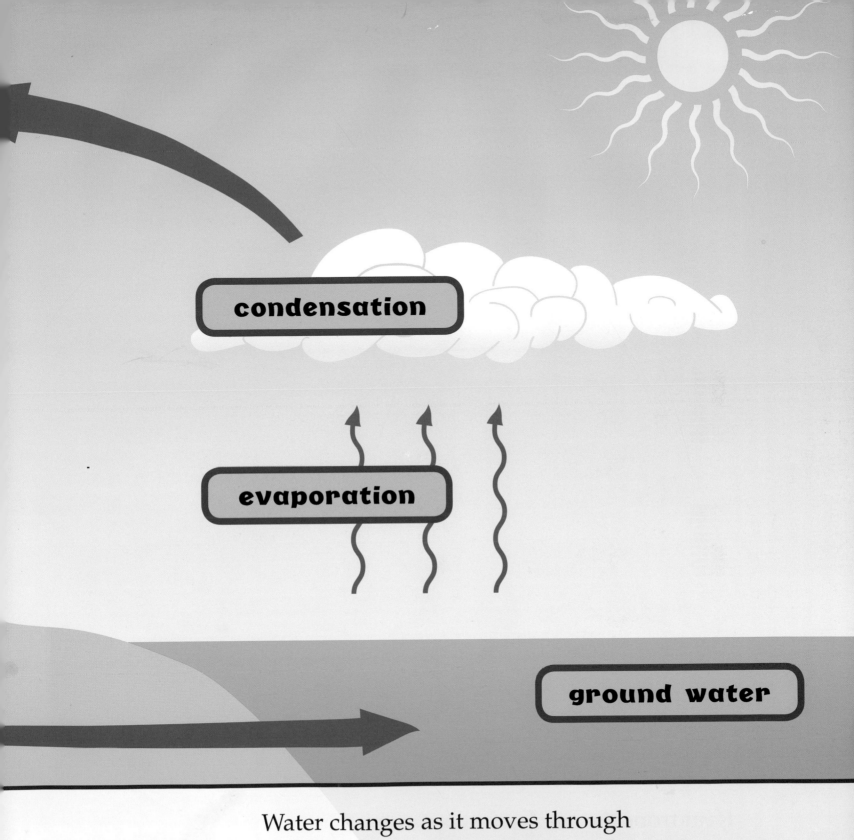

condensation

evaporation

ground water

Water changes as it moves through
the water cycle. The water cycle has
no beginning and no end.

Heat from the sun warms up water. The water
turns from a liquid into a gas. It evaporates.
The water vapor rises into the air. Water vapor
is all around you. It's a gas you can't see.

As water vapor rises, it cools. Cooling
causes the gas to turn back into a liquid.
This process is called condensation.

Condensation appears on a glass of cold water. It appears as dew on morning grass. On a cold winter day, you can see it on windows. Frost is frozen dew.

The tiny drops of water vapor get bigger as
they cool. You can see them as mist or fog.
Condensation also forms clouds.

Clouds are made of water droplets and bits of dust. As more water vapor cools, the clouds get heavy with water. Rain is on the way! When water falls from the clouds, it's called precipitation.

During warm weather, rain falls. During cold weather, water can fall as snow, sleet, or hail. Precipitation falls into rivers, lakes, and oceans. It seeps into the ground. It turns into ice on mountains.

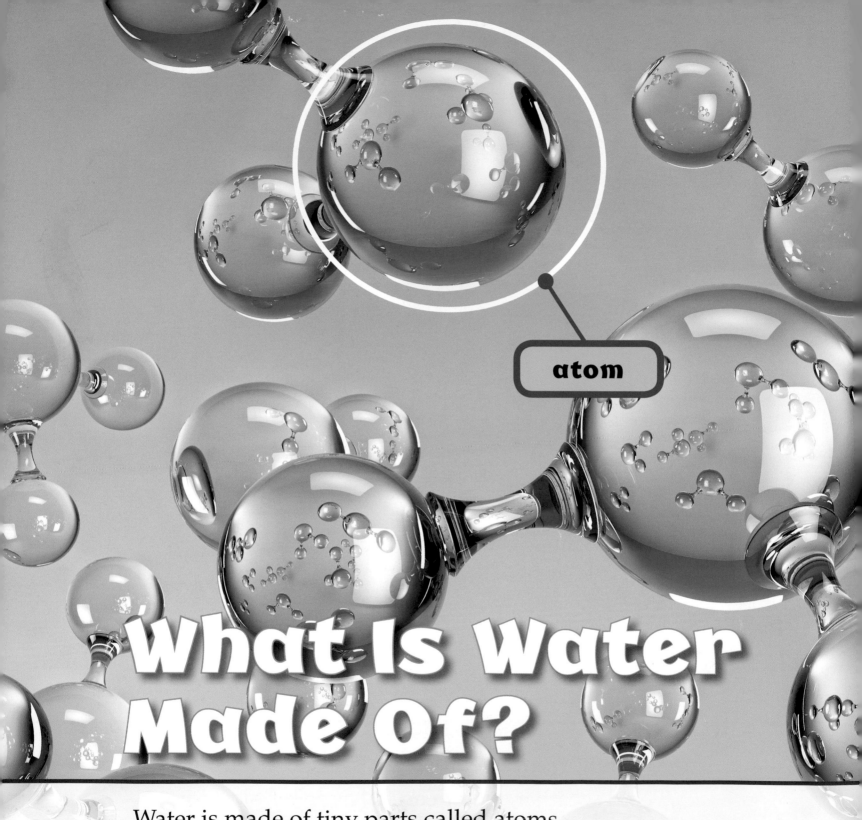

atom

What Is Water Made Of?

Water is made of tiny parts called atoms.
Atoms are too tiny to see.

molecule

Atoms are like building blocks.
They join together to make molecules.
Just one drop of water is made up of
millions of molecules!

Where Is Water Found?

You can find water almost everywhere.
Water covers more than 70 percent of Earth.

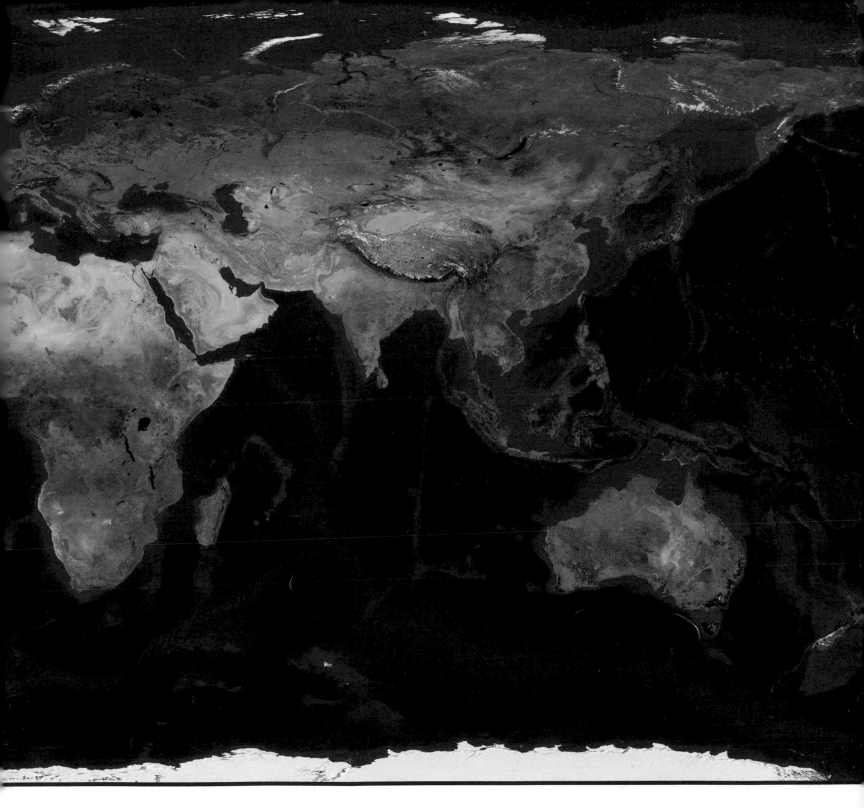

Water is used over and over again. It moves and changes form. But it never goes away. The same water has been on Earth for billions of years. The water you use today may have been drunk by dinosaurs!

What Is Water Used For?

Water is used for lots of things. You use it to wash your hands and clothes. You swim in it. You drink it.

Firefighters use water to put out fires. Farmers use it to grow crops. Cooks and bakers use water to make food.

Animals and plants need water too. Fish swim in water. Deer drink water from lakes and streams.

Flowers and trees need water to grow.
Their roots suck water from the ground.

Drinking Water

Water keeps you healthy. Be sure to drink about eight glasses of water each day. About 60 percent of your body is made up of water!

Only about 1 percent of Earth's water is good for drinking. Most water is salty ocean water. The rest is ice.

Waste from factories, farms, and toilets can cause water problems. So can litter. It may make water unsafe.

Cities clean their water. They make it safe for people to drink. But wild animals and plants don't have a way to clean their water. They need us to keep it clean.

Sharing Water

Use only as much water as you need. Take shorter showers. Turn off the water when you brush your teeth. Plant flowers that don't need much water.

We share water with everyone and
everyone and everything in the world. We also share it
with future people, plants, and animals.
Keep it clean!

Change It Up!

Water can be found in nature as a liquid, a solid, and a gas. Try this experiment to see how water changes from one form to another.

What You Need:

waxed paper

water

What You Do:

- Sprinkle a few drops of water on a piece of waxed paper. You can scatter drops by shaking your wet fingers over the waxed paper.
- Place the waxed paper in the freezer.
- After about 15 minutes, take out the paper. What has happened to the water droplets?

- Now place the waxed paper in sunlight or under a bright light. What happens to the water droplets now?
- Keep watching as the liquid drops seem to disappear. Where do the water drops go?

GLOSSARY

condensation—changing from a gas to a liquid

evaporate—to change from a liquid to a gas

hail—small balls of ice that form in thunderstorm clouds; hail falls from the sky

liquid—matter that is wet and can be poured, such as water

molecule—group of two or more atoms joined together

precipitation—water that falls from the clouds in the form of rain, hail, or snow

root—the part of the plant or tree that is below the ground

seep—to flow or trickle slowly

sleet—rain that freezes as it's falling and hits the ground as frozen pellets of ice

underground—below the ground

water cycle—how water changes as it travels around the world and moves between the ground and the air

water vapor—water in gas form; water vapor is one of many invisible gases in air

READ MORE

Linde, Barbara M. *The Water Cycle.* Where's the Water? New York: Gareth Stevens Publishing, 2016.

MacAulay, Kelley. *Why Do We Need Water?* Natural Resources Close-Up. New York: Crabtree Publishing Company, 2014.

Rustad, Martha E.H. *Water.* Little Scientist. North Mankato, Minn.: Capstone Press, 2014.

INTERNET SITES

FactHound offers a safe, fun way to find Internet sites related to this book.

All of the sites on FactHound have been researched by our staff.

Here's all you do:

Visit *www.facthound.com*

Type in this code: 9781515770800

Check out projects, games and lots more at
www.capstonekids.com

CRITICAL THINKING QUESTIONS

1. Name the parts of the water cycle. Hint: Use the picture on pages 6–7 for help!
2. You can find water almost everywhere. How much of the Earth is covered by water?
3. It's important to keep water clean. We share it with everything and everyone in the world. How can you keep water clean?

INDEX

animals, 20, 25, 27

atoms, 14–15

clouds, 5, 11, 12

condensation, 9, 10–11

drinking, 18, 20, 22, 23, 25

evaporation, 8

molecules, 15

plants, 20, 25, 27

precipitation, 12–13

raindrops, 4–5, 6

uses, 17, 18–19, 20–21, 26

water cycle, 6–7

water vapor, 8–9, 11, 12